Guidelines for Writing a Research Report

David Morris, Ph.D.
Associate Professor of Marketing
University of New Haven

Satish Chandra, J.S.D.
Professor of International Business and Law
University of New Haven

Copyright © 1993

 American Marketing Association
250 South Wacker Drive
Chicago, IL 60606-5819

Printed in the United States of America

ISBN # 0-87757-232-1

STRUCTURE OF A
RESEARCH REPORT

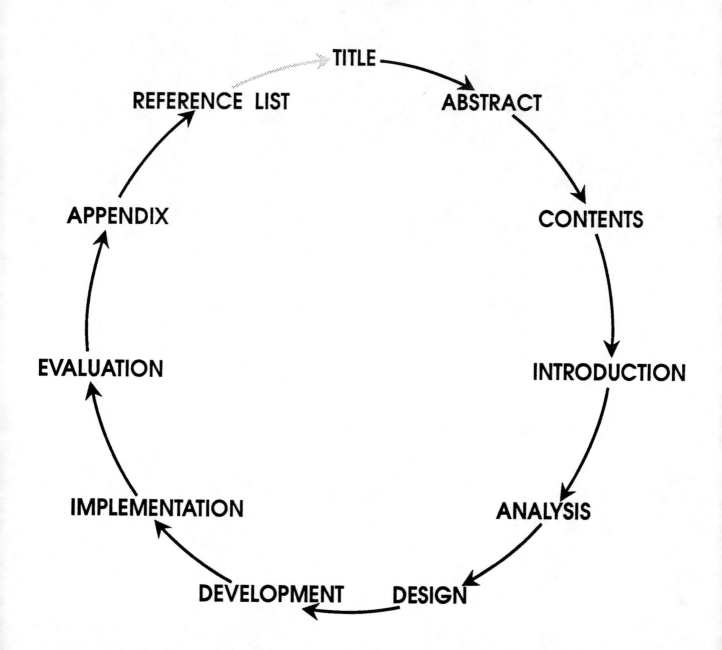

CONTENTS

FOREWORD

This book defines the basic steps used in writing a research report. The authors by no means presume that the treatment of the subject is exhaustive. However, we believe that the users of this book can improve dramatically their understanding of the requirements for writing a research report. The Guidelines is not meant to replace marketing research textbooks; it is an overview of the marketing research process. White space is provided on many pages for the users' notes and ideas.

This book contains very few samples of research because it is designed to deal with landmarks of structure. Use the "Structure of a Research Report" charts as a template to assess your research projects. The authors wish to thank Ms. Ginny Shipe of the American Marketing Association for her encouragement and support.

D. Morris

S. Chandra

STRUCTURE OF A RESEARCH REPORT

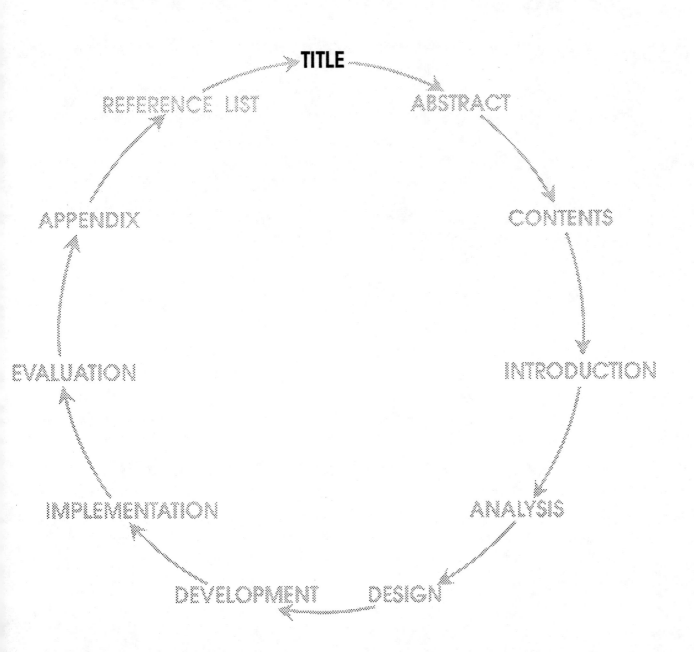

TITLE PAGE

The TITLE page should have the following information:

TITLE OF THE RESEARCH PROJECT

- The TITLE of the research project should spell out briefly the nature and the scope of the projected research.

- Capitalize the first letter of the first word, the first word after a colon, and all other words excluding articles, coordinating conjunctions and prepositions.

AUTHOR IDENTIFICATION

- Identify yourself and other members of the research team by name and designation.

  — Names may be either in alphabetical order or in the order of input.

  — Designation refers to the title(s) of the researcher(s).

Examples:

Satish Chandra, J.S.D.

David Morris, Ph.D.
Associate Professor of Marketing

Mary Harvey
Research Assistant

James Illing
Graduate Student, University of New Haven.

TITLE

IDENTIFICATION OF SPONSORING ORGANIZATION(S)

- In cases where the research project is conducted for a particular professor or organization, or funded by a sponsor, the name of such individual or organization should be included.

- The identification should be preceded by: Submitted to, *or* Prepared for, *or* Presented at.

DATE

- The date of submission or of the final preparation of the project

Use <u>The Chicago Manual of Style</u> for the layout of the title page.

See the next page for a sample of a TITLE page.

A TITLE page should not be numbered.

The Relevance of Zen: Marketing Theory and Practice

David Morris, Ph.D.
Associate Professor of Marketing
University of New Haven
West Haven, CT 06516
(203) 932-7348

Satish Chandra, J.S.D.
Professor of International Business and Law
University of New Haven

Presented at:

Global Marketing Association

March 2, 1997

STRUCTURE OF A RESEARCH REPORT

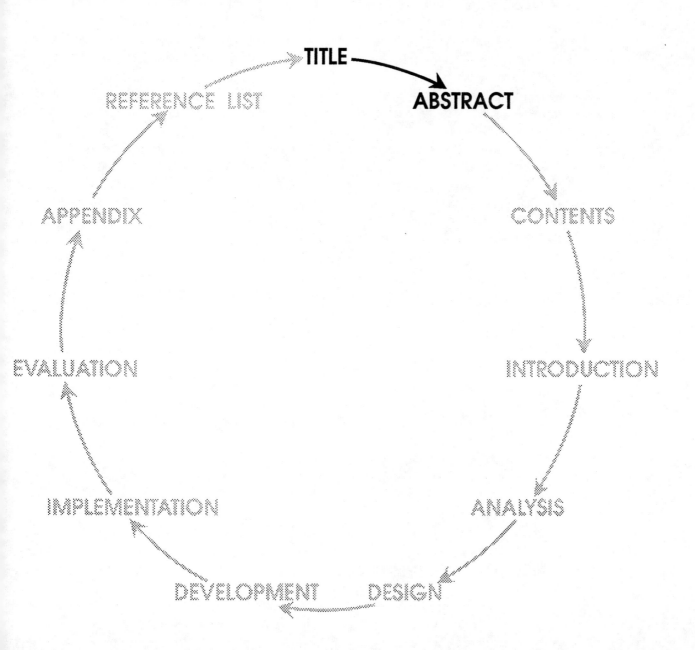

ABSTRACT

An ABSTRACT of the research project should deal with the following:

1.   The nature or general subject of the research

     • If the research project pertains to marketing management, it should state the specific characteristics of the study.

2.   The scope of the research

     • Describe the parameters of the research.

3.   The methodology used in the study

     For example:

     Statistical survey
        Interview
        Questionnaire

     Extrapolation using historical data

     Scientific experimentation

4.   Conclusions and recommendations

     The ABSTRACT:

          — should cover from one fourth to one third of a page.

          — is written after the research project is completed.

          — is organized into one paragraph.

          — appears on a separate page with the word "Abstract" centered at the top.

          — is single-spaced.

          — The ABSTRACT page is numbered in lower-case Roman numerals.

STRUCTURE OF A
RESEARCH REPORT

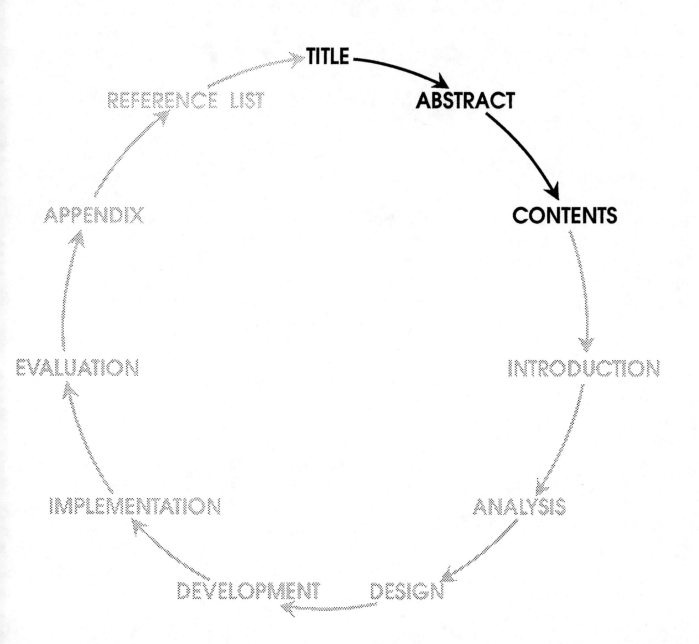

CONTENTS

- The CONTENTS help the reader find relevant material in the research report.

- The CONTENTS contain the following items along with the page number of each item:

- The CONTENTS also include subsections and their page numbers.

- The materials in the APPENDIX may appear in the CONTENTS or on a separate page. The first page of the APPENDIX is numbered in sequence with the other pages in the table of contents. Specific APPENDIX references are numbered A-1, A-2, A-3. This may be done for each page of the APPENDIX or for each separate document in the APPENDIX.

The CONTENTS page(s) is/are numbered in lower-case Roman numerals.

STRUCTURE OF A
RESEARCH REPORT

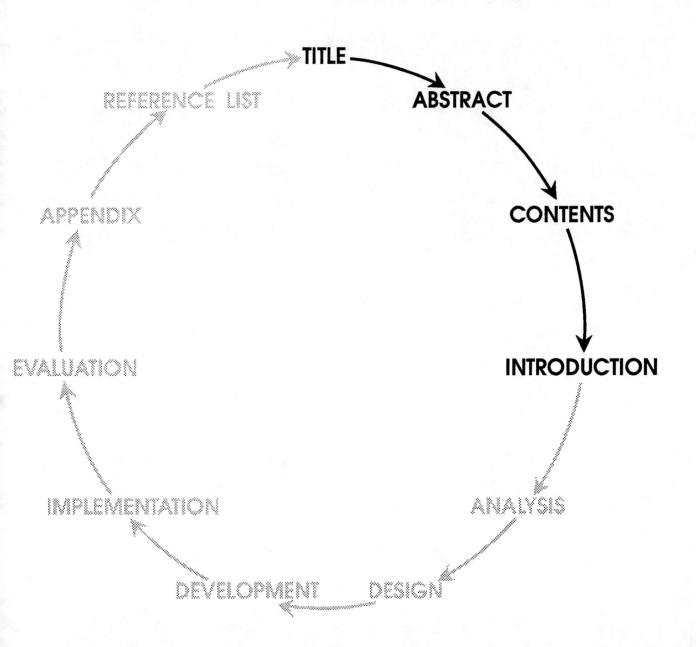

INTRODUCTION

- The INTRODUCTION provides a broader overview than the ABSTRACT and sets the stage for the subject of inquiry.

- The INTRODUCTION should include:

    1. Historical background of the subject.

    2. The methodology employed and its rationale.

    3. Broad interpretation of the results, conclusions and recommendations.

- As a rule, the INTRODUCTION should not exceed two pages.

- The INTRODUCTION is written after the research report is completed.

The text pages begin with Arabic numeral 1.

STRUCTURE OF A RESEARCH REPORT

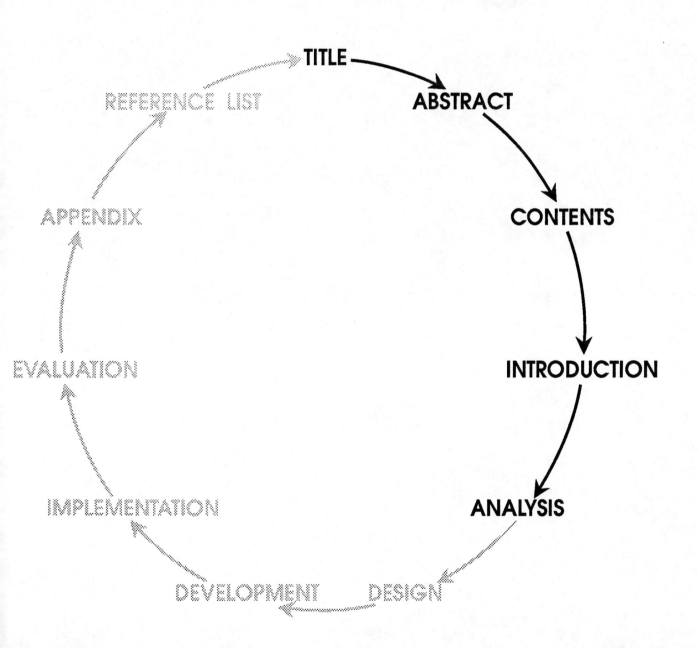

ANALYSIS

METHODS

The methods of business research include:

1. Historical

   - Data are collected from artifacts, scholarly publications, and other relevant sources. The study concentrates on historical developments.

2. Extrapolation

   - Relevant data are collected (generally from the recent past), and a projection is made for the future.

3. Current surveys

   - Data are collected through field work, personal interviews, telephone interviews, questionnaires, observations, mail surveys, and focus groups.

4. Causal studies

   - A dependent variable is a function of one or more independent variable(s).

   - A dependent variable is the effect and the independent variable(s) is the cause of the dependent variable.

     (SEE PAGES 20, 21)

The historical and extrapolation approaches use secondary data.

The current surveys and causal studies approaches use primary data.

PRIMARY DATA

Primary data are collected firsthand by the researcher.

Primary data can be:

- Internal:

    — Internal data are gathered from the organization to which the researcher belongs.

- External:

    — External data are gathered from sources outside the organization to which the researcher belongs.

SECONDARY DATA

Secondary data are collected by someone other than the researcher but are utilized by the latter.

Secondary data can be:

- Internal:

  — Internal data are collected from the researcher's organization.
  For example: from financial records, sales performance, cost of production, advertising, promotion, etc.

- External:

  — External data are collected from outside the organization.
  For example: from public documents, on-line sources, journals, magazines, newspapers and electronic media.

STATEMENT OF THE PROBLEM

This is the focus of the study.

- The solutions that have been offered so far are unsatisfactory; therefore, that particular problem needs further exploration to gain new insights. Most problems have sub-problems. These may be broken into multiple questions, as covered on page 17.

HYPOTHESES

The researcher should be precise in stating the hypotheses. The research project is intended as a tentative solution to the problem. In offering a tentative solution, the researcher will either support or refute a given hypothesis.

Examples of some research hypotheses:

a.   The mission statement of an organization describes its corporate culture.

b.   Antitrust laws inhibit corporate growth.

c.   Zen philosophy has contributed to quality production management.

Null hypotheses:

- are the research hypotheses written as negative statements.

- are a more efficient way to state your research questions.

- permit the researcher to reject a null hypothesis when any contrary evidence is found.

- when rejected, lead the researcher to accept the research hypotheses.

Researchers should discuss the problem studied in the project in the broad context. They need to survey the problem in the following contexts:

HISTORICAL

- Review of the history of the subject of the research:

    — Research projects that have been published

- Data pertaining to the project such as demographic surveys, market research, opinion polls, etc.

LITERATURE REVIEW

- Review of previous research projects on similar subjects

- Evaluation of similar research

- Current research pertaining to this project

- Any relevant material

DEFINITIONS

- Definitions of terms used in the research project

    — The definitions may be cited from reliable sources, such as <u>Webster's Third New International Dictionary</u> and/or scholarly publications.

    — The researchers are at liberty to define their own terms for the research; however, they must use these terms consistently throughout the report.

QUESTIONS

- What questions does the researcher attempt to answer?

    — Questions are derived from the statement of the problem.

    — The answers to questions provide the means to support or refute the hypotheses.

    — The selection of questions is based upon the criteria established for the research project.

    — For business research, the answers to the questions should lead to cost-effective decisions.

STRUCTURE OF A
RESEARCH REPORT

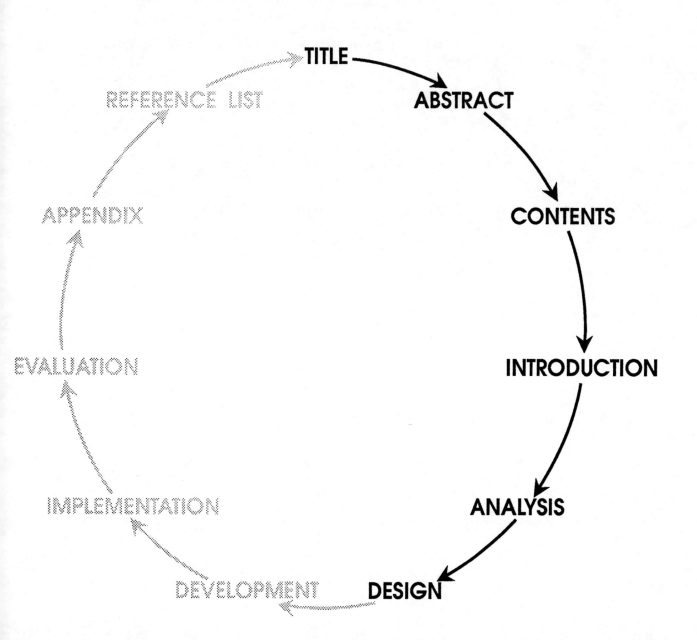

DESIGN

- The DESIGN section is also called methodology and/or experimental design.

- The DESIGN describes how the project is to be carried out.

- The DESIGN should conform to one of the approaches listed below:

  — Having identified the problem in the ANALYSIS section, the researcher should describe the DESIGN method (historical, analytical or conceptual) most appropriate for the research project.

HISTORICAL

In the historical method recent discoveries or technological innovations are compared with historical evidence.

ANALYTICAL

In this approach current data are obtained and analyzed to test the hypotheses. See a textbook on statistics for a more in-depth understanding.

CONCEPTUAL

In this approach the researcher observes a current phenomenon and evaluates it on a conceptual basis. For example, having witnessed the fall of an apple from a tree, Sir Isaac Newton conceptualized the idea of gravity. Many experiments, if not all, are derived from this type of serendipitous thinking.

SCOPE

- The researcher must identify the framework of the proposed study.

- Resource and time constraints, as well as the requirement for a pointed focus, compel the researcher to limit the breadth of the study.

VARIABLES

- Are generally applied to conceptual studies.

- Are divided into two categories: independent and dependent.

Independent variables (cause)

- Uncontrollable or external forces effect and/or affect change.

  — *For example:* the marketing manager has no control over the competition, the legal system, the cultural preferences of a customer at a given point in time.

  — *Another example:* gravity is an independent variable because it is beyond human control.

- A dependent variable may have a predictable reaction to change in an independent variable. This does not necessarily prove cause and effect.

VARIABLES

Dependent variables (effect)

- The variable the researcher wishes to explain.

- Elements controllable by the decision maker

  — *For example:* the marketing manager has control over the price that is charged for a product sold by his company.

  — In an experiment where life expectancy is the dependent variable, the independent variables could be life-style, genetics, or occupation.

- Research should identify the independent variable(s) [cause] in relation to the dependent variable(s) [effect]. Having done this, the researcher analyses the impact of the independent variables (cause) on the dependent variable (effect).

  — *For example:* the impact of antitrust laws (cause) on management desire to monopolize the market (effect).

After identifying numerous independent variables (causes), the researcher should select those independent variables (causes) which are more significant for the study. This is necessary because every study is conducted under various constraints, particularly time and money.

The dependent variable (effect) is the focus of the study because it is through that variable(s) that a decision maker attains the desired goal(s). Therefore, the research will be confined to measuring the impact of the selected significant independent variables (causes) on the dependent variables (effects).

Having measured the impact of the independent variable (cause) on the dependent variable (effect), the researcher advises the decision maker to manipulate the dependent variable to optimize the goal(s) of the organization.

STUDY

When the breadth of the study proves to have too large a universe, the researcher may select a representative sample from that universe.

SAMPLE SIZE

The size of the sample is determined by certain constraining factors such as methodology, time, money and available population. The researcher should justify the sample as conforming to the universe.

DATA

In a historical and extrapolation study, data are selected from particular secondary sources to test the hypothesis. Current surveys apply primary data, but in some circumstances these studies may also apply secondary data. Selection of cause variables will depend upon their significance. Each independent variable (cause) must be quantified.

Example:
- By using the multiple regression method, the impact of numerous independent variables (causes) on the dependent variable (effects) is analyzed. The results thus obtained are used to verify the hypothesis.

DATA COLLECTION

The study will indicate the method of data collection. Any unusual circumstance(s) affecting the study favorably or otherwise should be identified and documented. If the research is based upon a survey questionnaire, then the plausibility (validity and reliability) of the questionnaire should be adequately explained within the text. A copy of the questionnaire should be included in the APPENDIX.

VALIDITY

- Generally applied to conceptual studies.

- The extent to which a scale (questionnaire) is a true reflection of the variable(s) it is measuring.

CONTENT VALIDITY

The extent to which the content of a measurement scale (questionnaire) reflects all relevant variables to be measured.

CONSTRUCT VALIDITY

Can the result of the test be correlated with other similar tests? Do they measure the same thing? Are they different from one another? Does the test really measure the abstract concept it is supposed to assess?

PREDICTIVE VALIDITY

Are test scores reflective (predictive) of an individual's performance? For example, can a person who gets a high test score on an instrument that is supposed to predict the ability to sell actually sell?

RELIABILITY

- Generally applied to conceptual studies.

- How consistent or stable are the ratings generated by the scale (questionnaire)? Will you get the same results each time?

TEST-RETEST RELIABILITY

Will a given person achieve the same result on a scale each time that person is tested?

SPLIT-HALF RELIABILITY

If you split the test (questionnaire) into two sections, will the result on the two halves of the test (questionnaire) be the same?

COST/BENEFIT ANALYSIS

Every study is intended for implementation, which will incur certain costs. Therefore, every study should project the estimated costs and the estimated revenues or other expected benefits to be derived from the research. The expected benefits must far exceed the costs.

LIMITATIONS

The researcher should identify the limits of the study in terms of time, money, personnel, and other limiting factors.

STRUCTURE OF A
RESEARCH REPORT

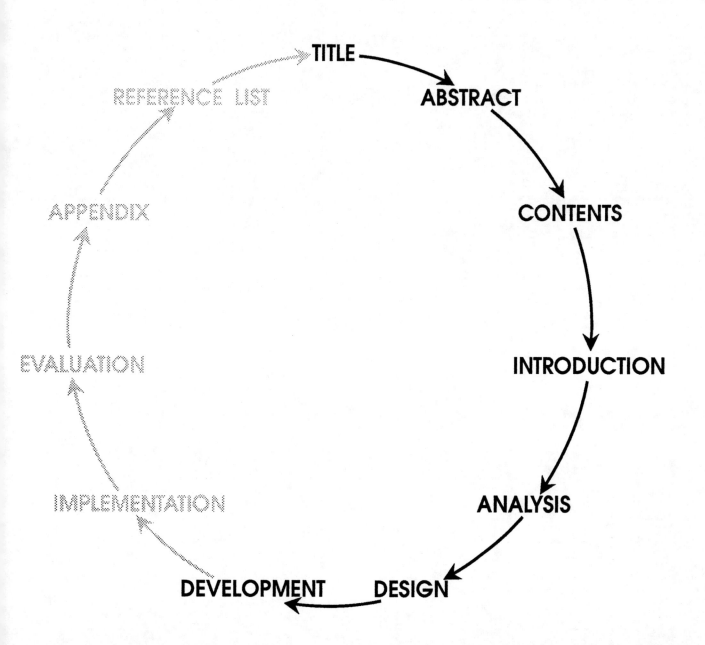

DEVELOPMENT

- All hypotheses that the researcher has identified should be tested, or developed, before IMPLEMENTATION.

PILOT TESTING

Testing is a critical and necessary factor in any research study. There are several methods for testing. One of the simplest test methods is to ask someone from the targeted population to read/test the questionnaire. While he or she is going through the questionnaire, minutely observe his or her demeanor particularly their body and facial expression. Go over the whole questionnaire line by line. Any pause or change in the reader's demeanor should be explored. For example, ask: Does that sentence make sense? What do you think the study is about? What do you think the question means? Why did you answer the way you did?

Having done so, repeat the same process again with someone else from the targeted population. Continue to refine and improve the questionnaire in this manner until confident of the quality of the pilot questionnaire.

Before embarking upon the general (questionnaire) survey, test it on a small group of the targeted population to elicit response. This approach is of immense value to the analysis of test-retest reliability.

TEST EXPERTS

There are those who show the questionnaire to experts before they test it on the particular targeted population.

STRUCTURE OF A RESEARCH REPORT

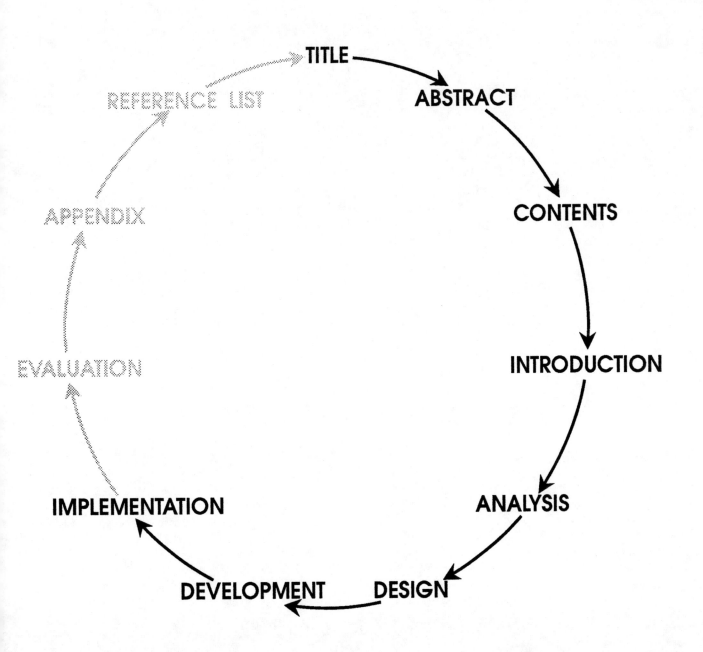

IMPLEMENTATION

- Do the study as DESIGNED and DEVELOPED in the earlier sections.

SUMMARY OF PROCEDURES

SUMMARY OF FINDINGS

- This section does not include any value judgements of the researcher; it simply provides a summary of what was done and what was found and may be presented using tables. See The Chicago Manual of Style for table construction.

- The researcher must make sure that his or her presentation represents a distillation of important items and is not merely a rundown of the detailed data. The data collected should appear in the Appendix section. The form in which this data is presented in the Appendix must insure the confidentiality of the respondents; therefore, the names and addresses of respondents must be deleted or substituted.

- The researcher records the activities that occurred when the research was conducted.

- This section also includes the information which the researcher has obtained through opinion surveys and questionnaires, etc.

STRUCTURE OF A
RESEARCH REPORT

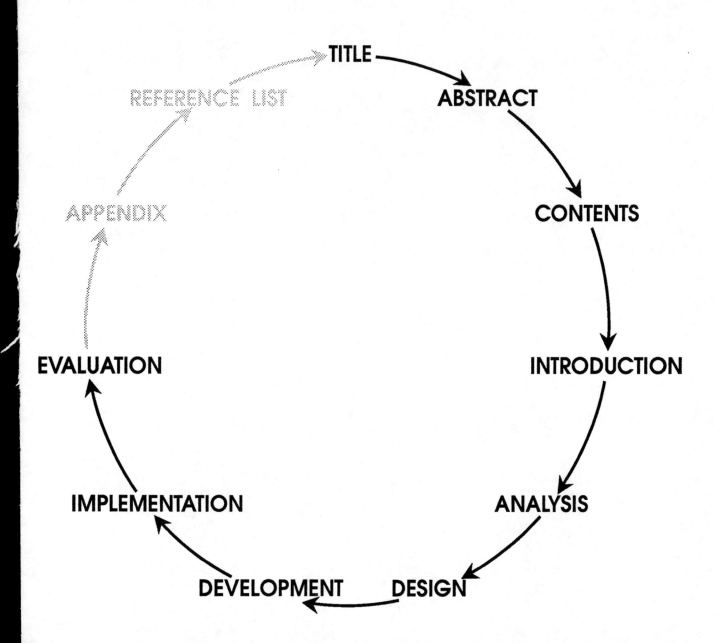

EVALUATION

The term EVALUATION is interchangeable with other terms: conclusions, summaries, findings, etc.

DISCUSSION

This section is where the researcher discusses and analyzes the study. The researcher is free to inject his or her own subjective interpretation of the study. The author's view is based on the results gained from the primary and secondary data, which may be presented using tables. See <u>The Chicago Manual of Style</u> for table construction.

The discussion section allows for subjective interpretation of the data. As a matter of fact, all decisions and conclusions have a certain element of subjectivity (perception) of the decision maker and the researcher. Two researchers may interpret the same subject matter differently. For example, one may perceive the cup to be half-empty; the other may perceive it to be half-full.

Some scholars have reinforced this concept by emphasizing "the myth of objectivity."

RECOMMENDATIONS

The research is intended to be cumulative and an aid to the decision maker in a particular organization. Therefore, by its very nature, it should identify the problem and find its solution. The researcher must take into account cost effectiveness in his or her recommendations.

FURTHER RESEARCH

In addition, the researcher should identify areas for further research.

STRUCTURE OF A RESEARCH REPORT

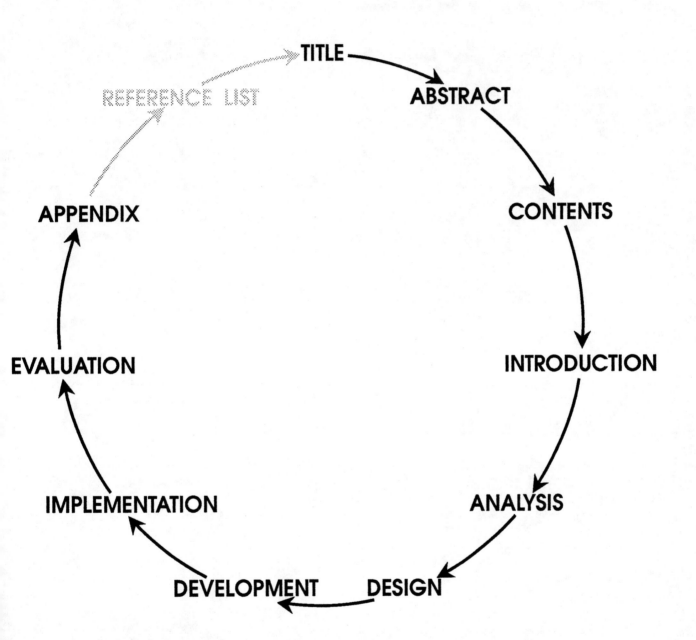

APPENDIX

The APPENDIX has many uses for the reader of the research report.

- Some materials which are relegated to the APPENDIX are explanations and elaborations. They are helpful to the reader in seeking further clarification of the study.

- The raw data included in the APPENDIX should be presented in a manner that guarantees the confidentiality of the respondents.

The APPENDIX may include:

— Sample survey questions

— Charts*

— Tables*

— Illustrations

— Summary data

— Letters

— Interview questions

When the above items appear in the APPENDIX, they are given an APPENDIX letter and number (A-1, A-2, A-3, etc.). Also, the source should be identified for each item. Check <u>The Chicago Manual of Style</u> for specific applications.

*Charts and tables that are placed in the APPENDIX are those that are deemed to have minor value; major charts and tables should appear in the text of the report.

STRUCTURE OF A RESEARCH REPORT

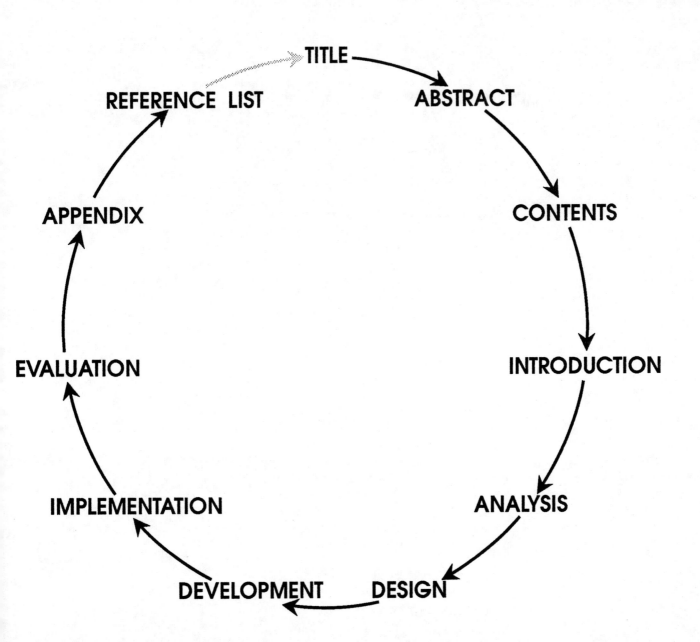

REFERENCE LIST

STYLE MANUALS

- There are numerous style manuals available for assistance in the writing of research reports.

- All references to anyone else's work must be acknowledged and cited properly. Failure to do so is plagiarism.

- For an in-depth review of the proper method for citing other people's work, see the following:

  — Ahmed, Saad, and David Morris. 1991. <u>Guidelines for business writing</u>. West Haven, Conn.: University of New Haven Press.

  — University of Chicago Press. 1982. <u>Chicago manual of style</u>. 13th ed. Chicago: University of Chicago Press.